70000037492

KT-431-707

£6.99

WITHDRAWN FROM STOCK

BEACONS OF LIBERATION
Fifteen Black Leaders

NG RESOURCES CENTRE
LLEGE

Shango Baku

H
HANSIB

Published by Hansib Publications in 2008
London & Hertfordshire

First Edition 1995
Second Edition 1996
Third Edition 2008

Hansib Publications Limited
P.O. Box 226, Hertford, Hertfordshire, SG14 3WY, UK

Email: info@hansib-books.com
Website: www.hansib-books.com

A catalogue record of this book is
available from the British Library

ISBN 978-1-906190-17-0

© Shango Baku

All rights reserved. No part of this publication may be
reproduced, stored in or introduced into a retrieval system,
or transmitted in any form, or by any means, electronic,
mechanical, photocopying, recording, or otherwise,
without the prior permission of the publisher.

Printed and bound in the UK

7000003 7492

Dedicated to Africa's freedom-fighters throughout time,
then and now...

FOREWORD

TWELVE OF THE BLACK HEROES AND HEROINES featured in this edition are depicted on a large mural adorning the mainspace at the Yaa Asantewaa Arts and Community Centre in Paddington, London. Three others have been added to this edition of Beacons of Liberation: Robert Wedderburn, Mary Prince, and Ira Aldridge.

Once known as 'The Factory', the Yaa Asantewaa Centre played a pivotal role in Black aesthetic and cultural development in Britain since the 1960's. Yaa Asantewaa, the famed warrior-queen of Ghana, fiercely resisted British colonisation, and was finally exiled to the Seychelles in 1902.

The thread of resistance, leadership, and commitment to change, connects the biographies summarised here. These achievers all rose from humble beginnings to become a light for millions. Several of them were killed for their beliefs. All showed exemplary fortitude and discipline in the face of adversity. All were courageous and determined in pursuing the goals they set for themselves.

Their combined stories, even in brief, are an impressive testimony to African achievement and social progress in the last half millennium. Together they speak for the cumulative momentum of African struggle and redemption from the 16th century to the present day.

Compiled & edited by Shango Baku
Artistic Director, CETTIE:
Cultural Exchange Through Theatre In Education,
58A Canonbury Road, London, N1 2DQ

Contents

BEACONS OF LIBERATION

Queen Nzinga
1582 – 1663

THE PORTUGUESE WERE AMONG THE FIRST Europeans to make contact with Africans in modern times. Initial encounters in the 15th century were amicable and on equal terms. The Portuguese were welcomed as traders. By the late 16th century they had established a foothold in the Congo. They were trading in slaves, and expanding their activities southwards into the territory of the Ndongo, whose King was known as the Ngola. The Portuguese mistakenly took this to be the name of the country (Angola).

In 1582 Princess Nzinga was born to the Ngola of Ndongo, who was engaged in a bitter struggle with the Portuguese. This war was to last for almost 100 years, and Nzinga would play a crucial role in her people's resistance to the European invaders.

On the death of her father in 1617, his eldest son Mbandi seized power killing all pretenders to the throne – including Nzinga's son. Mbandi was not only a murderer, but a coward who fled before the advancing Portuguese, abandoning the cherished Ndongo lands as he retreated into the interior. Nzinga's childhood had been spent in the shadow of continuous war with the Europeans. She inherited a fierce and courageous spirit from her father. When the time came to talk terms with the enemy it was she, not Mbandi, who made the long journey with her aides to the coastal fortress, which the Portuguese had built at Luanda.

Her meeting with the Portuguese Governor De Souza has passed into African legend, and was characteristic of Nzinga's

Queen Nzinga 1582 – 1663

astute leadership. Having been left standing in a large room while the governor sat in a plush chair (the only one available) Nzinga signalled to one of her handmaids, who arched her back for the princess to sit down. She was determined to meet the enemy on equal terms. When asked to return Portuguese captives who had been taken during the years of battle Nzinga agreed – on condition that the enslaved Africans who had been taken to Brazil could be returned in a fair trade-off. As this was not possible she demanded that her people's lands should be restored in exchange for Portuguese prisoners of war. A peace treaty was signed. Portugal promised to return their lands in exchange for help with the slave trade, and in repressing the warlike Jaga people.

De Souza may have meant to keep his part of the bargain, but there were growing demands from Lisbon and Brazil for more slave labour, and this factor dictated Portugal's African policy. When the usurper Mbandi died Nzinga assumed leadership of her people. Continuous attacks by the Portuguese forced her to withdraw from the plains into the highlands of Matamba, where she began to resettle her people in 1630. A supreme tactician Nzinga waged a fierce guerrilla war against the Portuguese, who installed a puppet chief in Ndongo in her place. Over the next 10 years she continued to harass the enemy forces with spasmodic raids, whilst creating new allegiances with the fearsome Jaga people. Her life seemed one long battle.

In 1639 the Dutch sent emissaries to her as they fought the Portuguese for supremacy in the slave trade. By 1641 they had taken Luanda, pushing the Portuguese into the interior, and fomenting rebellion against them by the Congo people in the North. From 1641-1648 the Dutch action helped Nzinga to re-establish her control in the plains of Ndongo. An uneasy peace was restored, but Nzinga knew that this was only a lull in the protracted war against the Portuguese.

When at last they returned with reinforcements from Brazil in 1648, they retook Luanda from the Dutch. Nzinga returned to her stronghold in the mountains.

The Matamba highlands became the home of the 'Angolans'. In the 1650's, tired of the long decades of war, Nzinga accepted overtures of peace from the Portuguese, and the ageing Queen slowly withdrew from the battlefront. Over the long years of war she had trained a new generation of fighters in the tactics of survival and jungle warfare. The future would be in their hands. While all the surrounding kingdoms had submitted to foreign rule the people of Angola had defended the precious gift of freedom. In 1663 aged 81, Nzinga died.

Three hundred years later, with Africa colonised and partitioned by European powers, Angolans were again locked in bloody conflict with an old enemy, Portugal. Their victory in this war was won with the same guerrilla strategies that Queen Nzinga had used centuries before.

Nanny
1670 – 1755

AFRICANS NEVER SUBMITTED MEEKLY TO THE injustices of slavery in the West. Slave revolts were increasingly common throughout the Caribbean and the Americas from the 16th century until emancipation was finally achieved in the mid-19th century.

The Spaniards first brought enslaved Africans to Jamaica in 1519. There was constant rivalry between European powers for the rich pickings of the slave trade. In 1655, the British captured the island from Spain. Enslaved Africans on the island took advantage of the ensuing confusion, and fled to the highlands of Jamaica where they could be free. These free Africans were known as Maroons.

The Maroons established orderly and well-defended communities in the Jamaican interior. Nanny was a great Maroon leader. A small, wiry woman with penetrating eyes, she came from the proud Ashanti tribe of West Africa. She and her brothers, Cudjoe, Accompong, Johnny, Cuffy and Quako, became leaders of the rebel Maroon towns.

Nanny controlled the east. She was renowned as a military strategist. Camouflaged by the natural forest, her troops would set deadly ambushes for the British soldiers who were unfamiliar with the terrain, and unprepared for guerrilla tactics. Nanny also organised raids on their plantations, seizing food and arms, and freeing enslaved Africans, who swelled the numbers of runaways under her command. She was a constant thorn in the side of the British. They suffered massive losses in supplies, captives, and morale. In the west,

Nanny 1670 – 1775

Cudjoe used similar methods to unsettle British occupation of the island.

The Maroon wars lasted from 1720 - 1739. Cudjoe finally signed a peace treaty with the British giving the Maroons land as free men. One condition of the treaty was that they would return runaway captives and help suppress further rebellion. At first Nanny refused to sign the treaty, urging the Maroons to continue to fight the British until all enslaved Africans on the island were free. In the end, she agreed to a truce with the British, as her people were exhausted and tired of fighting.

In Maroon lore, Nanny is remembered as a spiritual leader, and a healer accredited with superhuman powers. She preserved the culture of Africa in a new world, and kept her people mindful of their pride and dignity as free Africans. She was an inspiring example and role-model for Jamaican heroes who followed in her wake: Sam Sharpe, Paul Bogle, and Marcus Garvey.

Nanny died in 1755. She lies buried at Bump Grave in Maroon Town. In October 1975, her name was enshrined in Jamaica's roll of honour when she became the island's First National Heroine.

Robert Wedderburn 1762 – *c.*1833

Robert Wedderburn

1762 – *c.*1833

ROBERT WEDDERBURN WAS BORN IN JAMAICA in 1762. His father was James Wedderburn, a Scottish doctor who owned a sugar plantation on the island. His mother, an enslaved African woman called Rosanna, worked for Wedderburn. As was the custom (and indeed the law), a slave-owner could do whatever he liked with his own 'property'. Enslaved Africans were seen as chattel, i.e. goods that could be bought and sold, rented or hired out, used or abused in a manner befitting animals. So James Wedderburn forced himself upon Rosanna against her will. When she became pregnant he sold her to her former owner – possibly at a profit, since there was new life inside of her.

For the first 4 years of his life Robert was cared for by the kindly Lady Douglas, who had 'owned' his mother before she was sold to Wedderburn. But when Lady Douglas died his mother was sold again, and he was sent to Kingston, and placed in the care of his grandmother. As a young boy he witnessed many cruelties and injustices being inflicted on those around him. His grandmother was flogged severely when it was rumoured that she had used obeah (witchcraft) to cause the death of a White man. It was an incident that scarred the young Wedderburn's memory for life.

As soon as he turned 16 he seized the opportunity to board ship and work as a seaman. This was one of the few options for a better life, and Britain was advertising for young men to fill her merchant ships and Navy. In 1778 he arrived in England.

Here he worked as a tailor in St Giles, a ghetto area of London. He was part of a large community of Africans and other displaced people living in very poor conditions. A convert to Methodism, Robert Wedderburn was soon embroiled in the religious and political turmoil of the times. He was influenced by the Spenceans, who said that the land belonged to everyone. He compared the suffering of the poorer classes in Britain to the enslaved Africans in the Caribbean. Both had a common cause: they lived out their lives in the constant shadow of oppression. He saw the Haitian revolution (1797) as the perfect example of self-determination by Africans, and urged those who were crushed by the Corn Laws and other injustices of the British State to take up arms in their own defence. Wedderburn registered as a dissenting Minister and held meetings at his 'chapel' in Soho, attended by a wide range of free-thinkers from all walks of life. He emerged as a self-taught radical, a fiery orator, preaching revolution against both State and Church. His meetings were often monitored by government spies.

In 1819 he was arrested for seditious libel, but later released when his supporters paid £200 bail money. The following year he was again arrested, this time on the charge of blasphemy. He was sentenced to 2 years in Dorchester Prison, miles away from friends and family, approaching 60 years of age, with his health in decline. He was closely linked to the 'Cato Street' conspirators (1820). Among them was his friend and colleague William Davidson, the Black cabinet-maker who was hung publicly along with 4 others for their alleged complicity in a plan to blow up Parliament. Wedderburn, perhaps fortuitously, was in prison at the time. But he was deemed a live and present danger to the British State, and listed among the 33 most dangerous men in England.

In 1824 after his release from prison he published the autobiographical work *The Horrors of Slavery*. In 1831 at the age of 68 he was again incarcerated in Giltspur Street Prison on a charge of affray.

Wedderburn maintained that the rights of man are liberty and justice. Without these, human life was meaningless and empty. It was a common saying in his time that it was better to die as a man than to live as a slave. He saw it as a duty to fight for his God-given right to freedom, and encouraged others to do the same: Black and White. No record of his death has ever been traced.

Mary Prince 1788 – *c.*1883

Mary Prince
1788 - *c.*1833

MARY PRINCE WAS BORN AT BRACKISH POND, Bermuda, in 1788. Her family were the 'property' of Charles Myners. When Myners died she and her mother were sold to a Captain Williams. As a young girl Mary worked both as a domestic slave as well as in the fields, and was constantly flogged by her mistress. In 1806 she was sent to work on the salt-pans of Turk Island, and had to stand up to her knees in water for hours at a time.

In 1818 she was sold to John Wood, a plantation owner in Antigua, for $300. But she soon fell ill of the rheumatism, and had to walk with a stick. She met Daniel Jones, a former enslaved African who had bought his own freedom. They were married in December 1826. John Wood was furious when he found out that Mary had married, and gave her a severe beating with a horsewhip.

In 1828 John Wood and his wife took her as their servant to London. Soon after arriving in England she ran away and went to work for Thomas Pringle, a member of the Anti-Slavery Society. In 1831 Pringle helped her to publish her book, *The History of Mary Prince, A West Indian Slave* (1831). This was the first narrative of a Black woman to be published in Britain. Two prominent supporters of slavery in Britain claimed that her book contained a large number of lies. Mary and her publisher sued them for libel and won the case. An excerpt from her testimony of slavery is quoted here:

"I am often much vexed, and I feel great sorrow when I hear some people in this country say that the slaves do not need better usage, and do not want to be free. They believe the foreign people, who deceive them, and say slaves are happy. I say, Not so. How can slaves be happy when they have the halter round their neck and the whip upon their back? And are disgraced and thought no more of than beasts? And are separated from their mothers, and husbands, and children, and sisters, just as cattle are sold and separated? Is it happiness for a driver in the field to take down his wife or sister or child, and strip them, and whip them in such a disgraceful manner? - women that have had children exposed in the open field to shame! There is no modesty or decency shown by the owner to his slaves; men, women, and children are exposed alike.

Since I have been here I have often wondered how English people can go out into the West Indies and act in such a beastly manner. But when they go to the West Indies, they forget God and all feeling of shame, I think, since they can see and do such things. They tie up slaves like hogs, moor them up like cattle, and they lick them, so as hogs, or cattle, or horses never were flogged; and yet they come home and say, and make some good people believe, that slaves don't want to get out of slavery. But they put a cloak about the truth. It is not so. All slaves want to be free – to be free is very sweet.

I will say the truth to English people who may read this history that my good friend, Miss S--- is now writing down for me. I have been a slave myself. I know what slaves feel. I can tell by myself what other slaves feel, and by what they have told me. The man that says slaves be quite happy in slavery – that they don't want to be free - that man is either ignorant or a lying person. I never heard a slave say so. I never heard a Buckra man say so, till I heard tell of it in England. Such people ought to be ashamed of themselves. They can't do without slaves, they say. What's the reason they can't do without slaves as well as in England? No slaves here - no whips - no stocks - no punishment, except for wicked people. They hire servants in England; and if they don't like them, they send them away: they can't lick them. Let them work ever so hard in England, they are far better off than slaves. If they get a bad master, they give warning and go hire to another. They have their liberty. That's just what we want. We don't mind hard work, if we had proper treatment, and proper wages like English servants, and proper time given in the week to keep us from breaking the Sabbath. But they won't give it: they will have work – work – work, night and day, sick or well, till we are quite done up; and we must not speak up nor look amiss, however much we be abused. And then when we are quite done up, who cares for us, more than for a lame horse? This is slavery. I tell it, to let English people know the truth; and I hope they will never leave off to pray God, and call loud to the great King of England, till all the poor blacks be given free, and slavery done up for evermore.

Mary Prince became a high-profile icon for the abolitionist movement. Ironically, she herself was not allowed to speak publicly. Her narrative was sanitised for public consumption, and she was carefully 'mothballed' by her supporters. They used her to bolster their moral claims, but in no way saw her as a sister and an equal. Through her narrative we glimpse the depths of cruelty, immorality, and constant abuse that African women suffered at the hands of their masters. No record of her death has been found to date.

Sojourner Truth 1797 – 1883

Sojourner Truth
1797 - 1883

THE YEAR IS 1852. THE PLACE: AKRON, OHIO, America. This is a church where a convention on women's rights is being held. Some have travelled hundreds of miles to listen, or to speak on this burning issue. A few Blacks are sprinkled among this mainly White gathering. Because this is a women's rights' meeting, anyone is allowed to speak – man or woman, for or against the motion. But Black women very rarely attended such gatherings, and very few had ever dared to address a White audience.

Perhaps because it is a church, several White ministers take the pulpit and denounce equality for women. The appearance of Sojourner Truth, a silent, lonely figure at this convention, unsettles some of the participants, and they beg Frances Gage, the organiser, not to let her speak. Her reputation preceded her. There was a growing fear among women's groups that their cause could be damaged by closing ranks with the abolitionists, whose agenda was to end slavery. Frances Gage was undecided, and Sojourner had not yet asked to speak. During the conference-break Sojourner distributed copies of her book *The Narrative of Sojourner Truth*. But it was not until the second day, after many speakers had given their opinion, that she approached the lectern:

"Why, I feel so pleased t'day. I feel pleased t'day 'cause I's in a place where I feel safe. Ole Sojourner's right here in God's pulpit t'day. And I's goin' to speak the truth as I knows it.

I must confess I ain't so pleased to hear what I been hearin' at this convention. 'Cause we all know that we live in a Christian nation. Yeah! America is a Christian nation. But I had to spend the first thirty years of my life under every kind a suffrin' that all you good people can think of – at the hands of white Christian men. And when the Good Lord gat me out of it – why, I seen dogs in New York being petted and treated better'n slaves. Anyways, if I talk too much about myself you good people ain't goin' to need to buy my book. Yessir! Thank the Lord! Ole Sojourner's gonna need every penny she can git to keep doin' the Lord's work. And this voice of mine's gonna ring like a bell – up and down America – till we all git the freedoms that's ours by right.

'Cause the teachin' of the Bible is about liberation. It says in Isiah: I come to free those who's bound up in prison, and to loose the bonds of the captives. And I was taught by my mama as a child to pray to God for whatever I wanted. So I prayed to be free. I was born a slave. I been sold over and over to different masters. I been beaten within an inch of death with hot iron rods. But I kept that faith my mama give me, and I stand before you today a free woman. Thank the Lord!

So I know that captive look, even if it ain't got chains on it. I know that deep down hurtin' feelin' I seen on the face of so many women – black and white. 'Cause when it come down to it, oppression ain't got no colour. It's just that white men have made a great art outa it.

Now this Preacher done told us that women's got less intelligence than men. Well ole Sojourner gonna put that lie to rest. 'Cause I done writ a book - and the good Lord knows I's illiterate. I din never learn to read, but I know what's in that Bible he preachin' from. Ain't he never heard about Deborah – a woman who was one of the first prophets in Israel? Why, she judged the people when there weren't no king in Israel. And how she gonna be chief judge and ruler if she ain't intelligent? That's in the Book of Judges. And who ain't heard about Esther – a great woman who turned the evil judgement on her people upside down, and took them right outa bondage. That's the Book of Esther. And there were great Queens in history like Nefertiti, who was blacker than what I am, and led a great and mighty nation. And how she goin' to rule a mighty nation if she don't have intelligence in the nappy hair under her crown? That's the Book of History. Yessir! Thank the Lord!

Preacher, he go on to say women's weaker'n men. And aren't I a woman? Aren't I a woman? Look at me. Look at ma arm. Why, I have ploughed and planted and gathered into barns and no man could head me. And aren't I a woman? Ain't no man opened doors for me, or helped me into carriages, or walked a ten mile that I couldn't keep up with'm. So I'm sayin' sisters - half of what them Preachers is sayin' is wrong, and the other half ain't worth listenin' to. We's got to speak out against it, but we also got to keep proving our case.

When they took my son Peter and sold him to a Southern slave-owner in Alabama I was sore distressed, as any mother would be. But the Lord said to me: Isabella (that was my name back then) – He say, Isabella, don't just sit there sorrowing. Git up and git your son back. He's your'n – ain't no-one got the right to take him away. And I got me up and fought a legal fight in the courts of America. And the Lord give me back my son, Peter. You kin read all about it in this here book of mine. That's the Book of Sojourner Truth.

I's gonna leave you with one last thought. 'Cause the Preacher says Eve was the mother of temptation, and she done caused all men to fall. Ain't that somethin'? Ain't that somethin'? If the first woman God ever made was strong enough to turn the whole world upside down - all alone - these here together ought to be able to turn it back and git it right side up again. Now ole Sojourner ain't got nothin' more to say. God Bless you all!"

The convention erupted in applause. Sojourner Truth, a fearless and outspoken campaigner for Black liberty, had scored another victory.

Sojourner Truth was a woman who overcame the impossible odds of history and circumstance to emerge as the leading anti-slavery and women's rights' spokesperson of her time – and one of the greatest public speakers in American history. She was a confirmed pacifist. She believed that the minds and attitudes of men could be challenged and changed by powerful arguments and positive action. Her espousal of the women's rights' campaign came as a direct result of the injustices she had suffered as an enslaved African. Her life fulfilled a mission. She leaves us the legacy of an outstanding role-model who linked two great human rights' movements in a crusade for true liberation.

(Sojourner's speech at the Convention is adapted from research and written by CETTIE)

Ira Frederick Aldridge
1807 - 1867

IN OCTOBER 1825, A BLACK MAN TOOK CENTRE stage at the Royal Coburg Theatre (now known as the Old Vic) playing the role of Oroonoko in the *Revolt of Surinam* or *A Slave's Revenge*. The playbill advertising the show made reference to the actor being 'a man of colour', and made much of the authenticity of his performance in a Black and noble role.

But those who were attracted by the novelty of a Black actor on stage were in fact witnessing the rise of the first international Black 'superstar'. Ira Aldridge went on to become the most decorated actor of modern times. He was also an outspoken abolitionist in an era when slavery was endemic in the southern states of his native America.

Born in New York in 1807, Ira Frederick Aldridge was the son of freed slaves Daniel and Luranah Aldridge. His father was a Church minister who wanted his son to follow in his footsteps, but the young Ira chose the stage as a career. He seized the opportunity to travel to England in 1824. A year later he had already begun to make his mark on the London stage. He married an Englishwoman, Margaret Elizabeth Gill, in 1825.

Aldridge was mercilessly slated by the London critics for his performances in Shakespearean roles that had been the exclusive domain of White actors. The sight of a Black genius onstage playing the classics was too much for them. He was a thorn in the side of those opposed to abolition. He exposed the lie that Blacks were intellectually and morally

Ira Frederick Aldridge 1807 - 1867

inferior. The pro-slavery lobby and their press cohorts singled him out for vindictive attacks – even when he received standing ovations for his magnificent portrayals – especially in *Othello*. He brought passion and reality to audiences who had become used to the posturing and melodrama of Victorian theatre.

Undeterred, Aldridge overcame his detractors. Abandoning the London stage he toured widely throughout the provinces of England, Ireland, and then Europe, attracting awards and plaudits wherever he played. Such was his stature in Europe and in Russia that he performed Shakespeare in English with casts of players who spoke in their own language. He 'whitened' his face for roles such as Lear, Macbeth, and Shylock, but left his hands Black – ensuring that his audiences were aware they were watching an African performer!

His triumphs in Russia gave him iconic status during his lifetime. Some quotes from those who attended his performances are appended here:

" ... the celebrated Negro American actor ... was the lion of St Petersburg, and it was necessary to book several days in advance in order to obtain a good seat at one of his evening performances." *Theophile Gautier, French novelist*

"In my time I have never seen a better *Othello*. I advise you not to miss him, in order to understand about Shakespeare." *V.V. Stasov, Russian theatre historian*

"In 1858 the influence of Aldridge on our actors was tremendous. Martinov, Maximov, Sosnitsky, Karatygin, Grigoryev, Bourdin, Leonidov, were all in ecstasies over him and gave him an ovation to which he warmly responded, fully conscious that they wanted to learn from him; certainly the acting of many of them afterwards became simpler, livelier, and more thought-out ... " *Mrs E.Yunge, daughter of Count Tolstoy*

"Aldridge has nothing in common with these theatrical personalities from the West who have visited us in recent times. His qualities consist not in picturesque poses and gestures ... but a highly truthful understanding of art, a deep knowledge of the human heart, and an ability to feel the subtlest spiritual movements indicated by Shakespeare and to bring them to life before the public – that is what constitutes the essence of his acting." *B.N.Almazov, Russian critic*

When at last he returned to London the West End stage could no longer afford to deny him. Aldridge had taken Shakespeare to places where no British actor had been before. His former detractors had become admirers.

Ira Aldridge died while on tour in Poland in August 1867. He was buried with solemn dignity in Lodz, where the whole city turned out to mourn the passing of the great tragedian. To this day his grave is carefully maintained by the Society of Polish Artists of Film and Theatre. He remains an outstanding example of victory over adversity, prejudice, and institutionalised racism. He was also a forerunner of 'naturalism' in modern acting technique. It is rumoured that Stanislavsky, the accredited author of 'method-acting', may have seen Aldridge on stage in Russia as a young boy.

In 2007, the bicentenary of his birth, several scholarly books were written in celebration of Aldridge. And his star, in eclipse for many years, began to shine again.

Harriet Tubman
1820 - 1913

HARRIET TUBMAN WAS BORN INTO SLAVERY IN 1820 on the Eastern Shore, a peninsula on the Atlantic seaboard of America in the state of Maryland – the most northerly of the southern slave states. The Mason-Dixon line was an imaginary boundary drawn between the northern states where Blacks were free, and the southern states where slavery was widespread. Born within 100 miles of the freedom line Harriet Tubman was destined to become the Black Moses who led her people out of bondage to safety in the North.

Harriet was one of eleven children born to enslaved African parents, Harriet Green and Benjamin Ross, the 'property' of a Maryland slave-owner called Edward Brodas. Maryland and Virginia were breeding-grounds for enslaved Africans who were sold 'down the river' to the more southerly states such as Alabama, Mississippi, Georgia and Louisiana. The lucrative cotton plantations in the Deep South depended on slave labour. After the abolition of the slave trade in 1807, slavery continued unabated in the southern states – supplied by Maryland and Virginia, who kept producing fresh labour markets for the cotton-fields.

Enslaved Africans could be rented or sold like any other commodity. From the age of five Harriet Tubman was regularly rented out by Brodas to Whites in Maryland for a variety of menial jobs that endangered her life. One involved standing in icy water for hours watching muskrat traps for her master. As a teenager she worked outdoors splitting fence-rails and loading timber onto a wagon.

Harriet Tubman 1820 - 1913

Though it was back-breaking work she enjoyed the open air more than the households of cruel masters and mistresses, who would use the rawhide whip on a slave's back at their slightest whim and fancy.

In 1835 she was struck on the forehead with an iron weight aimed at another enslaved African. For weeks she remained in a coma, and it was several months before she could walk without assistance. She never fully recovered from that blow. Her life thereafter was plagued by sleeping fits and sudden blackouts. The dream of escaping to freedom haunted her sleep. But fear kept most enslaved Africans in check. If recaptured – and many were – runaways were mercilessly punished.

In 1849 Harriet got word that she was to be sold to southern plantation owners. She decided that the time had come. The abolitionist movement was picking up momentum in the North. William Lloyd Garrison, a White journalist, championed the cause of abolition in his newspaper, *The Liberator.* Frederick Douglass, a Black man who had escaped from slavery in 1838, became a leading speaker on abolitionist platforms. The northern sympathisers had set up a network of safe-houses where escapees could be secreted temporarily on their flight to freedom. The system came to be known as the 'Underground Railroad'. Harriet got wind of it. When she at last fled from her master in 1849 she made contact with this 'chain of hope' that helped her on her trek across the Mason-Dixon line to freedom in Pennsylvania.

During the next 10 years Harriet Tubman became the main conductor on the Underground Railroad, leading hundreds of enslaved Africans, including members of her family, along a hazardous road to freedom. Later she boasted that she never lost a passenger. She had the guile of a military genius, often disguising herself as a man to escape detection as she herded frightened bands of freed Africans through dark forests and swampland, on foot, by boat, cart, or any other means available.

By 1856 Harriet Tubman was the most wanted woman in the southern states. A reward of $12,000 was offered for her capture, but the wily Harriet always remained one step ahead of her pursuers. On one occasion while travelling by train she held up a newspaper to her face, and slowly turned the pages as if she was studiously reading. The bounty hunters who had been trailing her turned away, knowing that the woman called 'Black Moses' could neither read nor write. Harriet praised God that she had held the newspaper the right way up!

Her trust in God was absolute, and this seemed to endow her with supreme courage in all the dangerous exploits she undertook. She also carried a revolver and was prepared to use it.

In the late 1850's the North and the South became increasingly polarised on the slavery issue. The pro-abolitionist Lincoln was elected President in 1860, and the Southern states broke away and became Confederate.

At the outbreak of war in 1861 Harriet Tubman lent her skills and knowledge of the South to the Unionist cause, acting as a nurse and a spy for Northern troops. Known to White commanders as 'General Tubman', she led a daring raid into Confederate territory freeing 750 enslaved Africans who enlisted with the North – as did thousands of others who deserted the plantations.

The end of the civil war (1865) signalled the end of slavery and the beginning of a new struggle for Blacks in America. Harriet returned to New York where she was sold a house by her abolitionist friends. Tired and penniless, she had to fight for her rightful earnings from the army. She survived by cultivating fruit and vegetables in her small garden and selling them to neighbours. Sarah Bradford, a New York writer, penned her autobiography in 1867/68, and the proceeds from sales helped to alleviate her poverty. She was able to feed her family and many others who came to her door in need.

Harriet Tubman lived out her remaining years in some comfort, entertaining visitors, telling tales of her exploits, and setting up a home for sick and needy Black people. In 1897 Queen Victoria awarded her a silver medal and invited her to England. She did not go, but the Queen's letter was a keepsake she fondly treasured. In 1911 she moved into the home she had founded. To the end of her days in 1913, like Moses in Deuteronomy, her mind was clear and her force unabated. Frederick Douglass had written to her in a letter in 1868:

"I know of no-one who has willingly encountered more perils and hardships to serve our enslaved people than you have."

Marcus Garvey 1887 - 1940

Marcus Garvey
1887 - 1940

MARCUS MOSIAH GARVEY WAS BORN ON August 17th 1887 in St Ann's Bay on the North Coast of Jamaica. His parents were descendants of the Maroons – Africans who had escaped from slavery and established self-governing territories in the highlands of Jamaica during the 18th century. Racial pride and an independent spirit were traits that would mark the life of Marcus Garvey, perhaps the most influential Black leader of the 20th century.

In 1901 Marcus Garvey left school at the age of fourteen to take up an apprenticeship as a printer. Four years later he moved to the capital, Kingston, where he soon became involved in workers' struggles for better pay and working conditions. Wherever he saw injustice he was an outspoken and fearless critic of the oppressor.

In 1910 he travelled widely in Central and South America in search of work. He saw everywhere the recurring spectacle of fellow Caribbean migrant workers living in wretched conditions on low pay. In 1912 Marcus journeyed to Britain. The 'Mother Country' still controlled the former slave-colonies, whose peoples were now economically exploited and destitute. Perhaps here he could find justice. London was a meeting place for Black intellectuals and seamen from all over the globe. Garvey found time to study, to exchange ideas, and to write for the *African Times and Orient Review*, a newspaper reflecting the views and conditions of oppressed people in Africa and Asia.

On his return to Jamaica in 1914, Marcus launched the United Negro Improvement Association (UNIA). But he soon found there was no money in Jamaica to further the cause of the Association, and it was difficult for impoverished Blacks to appreciate the programmes of the UNIA which focused on Black history and dignity.

In 1916 Marcus left for America to link with leaders in the Black struggle and to broaden the base of his organisation. He soon emerged as a powerful public speaker at rallies and gatherings in many cities where Black people were denied basic rights. He established the UNIA, which quickly spread to several American cities. By 1918 there were 30 chapters of the association with over 2 million active members. In that year the Negro World was launched as the official voice of the UNIA. The magazine was circulated throughout the Americas, the Caribbean, and Africa. Marcus Garvey became the most important Black figure in the world. He was a constant threat to White supremacists in Europe and America, who feared his growing popularity and influence.

In 1919 the UNIA launched its major project the Black Star Liner – a Black-owned shipping company that was intended to link the Black world. The following year, the first international conference of the UNIA was held in New York. Over 20,000 delegates attended. For the opening ceremony Garvey orchestrated a magnificent display of 'the Black nation' in a procession through the streets of New York, with section after section of brightly uniformed groups representing the army, nurses, the navy, auxiliaries, and youth corps, followed by music bands. Garvey's call was for 400 million Black people worldwide to come together and understand their common past and their present strength, in order to create a unified future. His best-known slogans were:

"One God, One Aim, One Destiny", "Africa for the Africans - at home and abroad", and "Up! You Mighty Race!"

In 1922 the American Government, fearing the growing power of Garvey, brought charges of mail fraud against him regarding the mismanagement of Black Star Liner stocks. In 1923, he was convicted and sentenced to five years imprisonment in Tombs Prison, Atlanta. A great outcry from the Black community led President Coolidge to commute his sentence in 1927. Marcus was seen as a dangerous man and was deported to Jamaica on his release. There, he received a hero's welcome with thousands lining the streets for his return, but he would never again command the influence he did in previous years.

Marcus Garvey continued to press for the rights of Black people in London, Paris and with the League Of Nations (forerunner of the United Nations). But the voice that had stirred millions of Black people the world over now attracted only small audiences. Unsuccessful in the local elections in Jamaica, he left for Britain in 1935 and resided there till his death in 1940. He was buried in Kensal Green, Paddington. His body was exhumed and taken to his native Jamaica in 1964, where he was posthumously awarded the status of First National Hero.

The influence of Marcus Garvey spread far beyond his country and his time. Great African leaders – such as Jomo Kenyatta, Kwame Nkrumah, George Padmore, CLR James, Walter Rodney, and Malcolm X, all testified to the profound effect that the philosophy and work of Marcus Garvey had on their lives. Though he never set foot on African soil he gave Africans a clear directive to look to their origins with pride, and prophesied that the time of deliverance was at hand.

Queen Mother Moore 1898 - 1996

Queen Mother Moore
1898 - 1996

THE LEGENDARY QUEEN MOTHER MOORE WAS born in Louisiana in 1898. Life in the Deep South of America had altered little since the days of slavery. Her mother died when she was three years old, the eldest of three girls. Her grandfather was lynched, and she herself witnessed a lynching at the age of five. Her politicisation could not have begun at an earlier age.

As a teenager she was heavily influenced by the teachings of Marcus Garvey and later became a UNIA activist, speaking on street corners in Harlem. She recalls an incident in 1918 that changed her life:

> "The police wouldn't let Garvey speak but we demanded that he speak. He came, and the police filed into the meeting hall man to man along the benches and across the platform. Garvey said: 'My friends I want to apologise for not speaking last night. The reason I didn't was because the Mayor of the city of New Orleans allowed himself to be used as a stooge for the Chief of Police'. The Chief jumped up on the platform and said 'I'll run you in!'

> When he did that everybody stood on the benches, and we all had guns and ammunition, and we pulled our guns out. I had two guns, and I was just a young girl. If you envisage two or three thousand people with guns in the air saying 'Speak, Garvey, Speak!' And Garvey said: 'As I was saying ...' And the police filed out of the hall like little puppy dogs with their tails between their legs. They got red like lobsters. From then on I found myself working eight days a week,

twenty five hours a day in the United Negro Improvement Association's struggle for our freedom."

Her activism in the Black struggle in America was to span the next sixty-five years during which she immersed herself in politics, was a tireless organiser of Black protests, and founded several associations for the advancement of the poor and oppressed. Among these were the Universal Association of Ethiopian Women, which helped impoverished families to obtain state benefits, the Harriet Tubman Association for domestic workers, and the African Historical Monument Project. She led rent strikes, food boycotts, workers' protests, sit-ins for better schools, and defence campaigns for Blacks who were victimised by America's corrupt judicial system. She addressed conferences, rallies, colleges, and mass meetings worldwide. She was a guest of the Organisation of African Unity, and was received by Heads of State in several African countries – notably Zimbabwe, and Ghana where she was dubbed Queen Mother of the Ashanti tribe. In the 1950's she joined the Communist Party but was soon disillusioned by its naive policy regarding 'negroes'.

> "I soon found out that the Communists weren't going my way because they insisted that we were 'Negroes' and I had questions about that. Where did Negroes come from? Why is it that China produces Chinese, Japan produces Japanese, France produces Frenchmen, England produces Englishmen, how could Africa produce 'Negroes' and not Africans ... A Negro is an imbecile, a concoction that was made by the slave master to do his bidding for him and who would function like a zombie. A Negro can't scrutinise, can't analyse, he is just incapable of looking at his situation and understanding what it means. He has been programmed to be something other than himself".

She also began to lobby for Reparations in view of the

immense damage and dislocation Black Americans had suffered during and after slavery.

> "The idea of reparations began to form in my mind about 1950, when I really became conscious of the injury, the damage, that they had done to us. This country owes us something, and we have passed over that whole epoch without a basic demand. In this country they made us citizens without our consent and in violation of our human rights".

In 1981 Queen Mother Moore visited Britain as guest of a Rastafari organisation the Tree of Life. Her advice was:

> "The Rastas have a philosophy of returning to the motherland, but I say that you should go with your reparations. You don't need to start from scratch – you have to claim what is yours".

In a lifetime that kept abreast of decades of continuous and changing struggles for Black liberation, Queen Mother Moore's outstanding example of social activism and political action gave substance to her titles as Mother and Queen. She extended the tradition of Sojourner Truth, Harriet Tubman, and other Black women who committed their lives to uplifting poor and downtrodden people everywhere. In one of her addresses in Britain she said:

> "We have some serious business to take care of – the business of our liberation, the liberation of the millions of Africans scattered throughout the world, and the more than 300 million Africans who perished crossing the Atlantic during slavery – the middle passage – the most horrific condition ever known to mankind. Others have suffered a 'hollow-cost', but we have suffered a hell-of-a-cost."

Kwame Nkrumah 1909 - 1972

Kwame Nkrumah
1909 - 1972

BORN IN 1909 IN A SMALL VILLAGE IN THE British Gold Coast, Kwame Nkrumah was destined to become one of the leading African political figures of the 20th century. He spearheaded the nationalist movement from colonialism to independence – not just in the Gold Coast (now Ghana) but throughout Africa.

As a young student Nkrumah showed great promise and was appointed a teacher at his local school at the age of 17. A year later he enrolled at the Government Training College in Accra, capital of the Gold Coast. His studies made him acutely aware of Africa's problems under colonialism. European countries controlled the lives of Africans in the post-slavery period. African economies were tied to European industries. The vicious cycle of exploitation of Africa's raw materials for capital gains in Europe was crippling the continent. The young scholar travelled to the USA in 1935. Here he was to spend the next 10 years of his life, studying, working, and becoming increasingly involved in the plight of Black Americans whose living standards belied their status as equal citizens of America.

Kwame Nkrumah earned many honours as a student and as a teacher in the USA. He also became involved in political activities and debates on Africa's future, speaking at public rallies and in churches as a 'Christian nationalist'. Like many Black leaders of his time, he confessed that Garvey's writings had helped to shape his political thought. Nkrumah became more and more certain that the time was right for Africans to govern themselves. Independence from the stranglehold of European dominance would become his life's work.

From the USA Nkrumah went to Britain in 1945 with the intention of continuing his studies. But here he became embroiled in the Pan African movement, meeting such figures as George Padmore, W.E.B.DuBois, and others. In his absence from Ghana the independence movement had grown. His name was widely circulated as a possible future leader of the country. In 1947 he was invited to return to Ghana to head the emergent UGCC (United Gold Coast Convention), an organisation advocating greater self-government. Nkrumah accepted, but his radical views soon led him to form a new party in 1949 – the CPP (Convention People's Party) with a more revolutionary agenda, using non-violent means to achieve self-rule. Limited self-rule was granted in 1951.

Nkrumah increasingly pressed for full independence in the years that followed. At last the British acceded to his demands in 1957. The Gold Coast became Ghana, one of the first sub-Saharan states to achieve independence from a colonial power. A political strategist, Nkrumah moved from West to East in search of help to develop his country. His ambivalence and outspokenness angered Western powers and members of his own party. His vision of Africa stretched beyond the borders of Ghana, embracing a much wider co-operation between African nations. This, too, was misunderstood by many.

Ousted by a coup while abroad in Vietnam in 1966, Nkrumah spent the remaining years of his life in exile in Guinea. He was offered co-presidency of the former French colony by his friend, President Sekou Toure. He was able to write, advise, and consult with leading figures in African and world affairs during these years. Today he is remembered not only as Ghana's first President, but as a founding father of the OAU (Organisation of African Unity) and as a nationalist whose views influenced the future of the continent.

Claudia Jones 1915 - 1964

Claudia Jones
1915 - 1964

BORN IN PORT OF SPAIN, TRINIDAD IN 1915, Claudia Jones moved to New York with her parents in 1923 at the tender age of eight. She was a gifted student and won the Theodore Roosevelt Award for Good Citizenship at the Junior High School she attended. In 1927 her mother died from overwork, collapsing over her machine in a New York clothes-making factory. Claudia could never forget this tragic loss. It brought home to her the cruel reality of life for Black people in America. Her life's work was dedicated to improving the living conditions of Blacks and working-class people throughout the world.

As a young woman seeking employment in the 1930's she continued to encounter racial discrimination at every turn. Her search for a philosophy that would combat racism in America led her to Communism (like other Black Americans of her time), and in 1933 she joined the Young Communist League (YCL).

Her work as editor of the YCL's newspaper brought her into contact with many young Black people, who she helped to organise in the struggle for employment and equal rights. A tireless campaigner, she became involved in the fight to free the 'Scottsboro Nine' – black youths accused of raping two white women. She also threw herself into the struggle for women's rights, having had first-hand experience of the living and working conditions of Black women in Harlem. Many of them were unemployed, in detention centres, or domestic servants. Her great hope was for a socialist revolution that would liberate America's working-class, and guarantee the full emancipation of women – Black and White.

In the mid-1940's Black soldiers and servicemen who had fought for America in World War 11 (1940-1944) returned home to find themselves still denied their basic rights as citizens of the USA. The anti-racist struggle intensified – and so did the repressive measures taken by the State against Black activists and communists. Claudia Jones, like the great American singer, Paul Robeson, became a victim of the McCarthy witch-hunt of the fifties. She was arrested in 1951 and charged with 'un-American activities'. Her trial dragged on from early 1952 to March 1953 when she was finally convicted and sentenced to a year's imprisonment. After several unsuccessful appeals she was imprisoned in 1955, despite ill-health and a strong international lobby on her behalf. She was deported to Britain on release from prison in 1956.

Claudia, a seasoned campaigner, immediately identified with the struggle of Britain's Black community. She founded the *West Indian Gazette* in 1958, the year in which the Notting Hill Gate race-riots exploded. With Amy Ashwood Garvey, widow of Marcus Garvey, she set up a committee to assist Blacks arrested while defending themselves against racist attacks.

In the next eight years the *West Indian Gazette*, running on a shoe-string budget, became the voice of Britain's growing Black communities from the Caribbean, Asia, and Africa. With the support of performers such as Paul Robeson, Nadia Cattouse, Corinne Skinner-Carter and Pearl Prescod, who helped raise funds for the paper, the Gazette continued its vanguard defence of human rights. Claudia spoke at anti-racist demonstrations, Trade Union meetings, and anti-apartheid rallies up and down the country. She inspired the first carnival celebrations in London in 1959. She visited

Japan, the Soviet Union, and in 1964, China, where she met with Communist Leader, Mao Tse Tung.

In 1964 she died in her sleep on Christmas Day, having suffered a stroke brought on by a heart condition and unstinting work. She is buried in Highgate Cemetery, London, next to the grave of Karl Marx. A beautiful and vibrant woman, Claudia Jones championed the cause of deprived communities in America, Britain, and across the world. Throughout her life she maintained a vision of international solidarity for the betterment of working-class people everywhere. She helped create mechanisms of defence against state oppression and entrenched racism. In the words of Paul Robeson, she was able to "contribute greatly to that movement which has emerged so powerfully in our time – the colonial liberation struggles which are helping to remake the world ..."

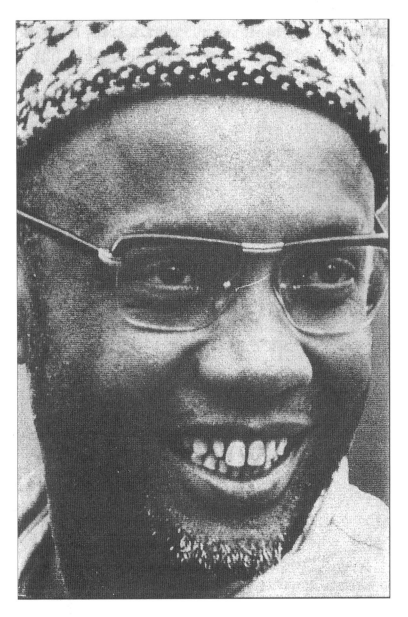

Amilcar Cabral 1924 - 1973

Amilcar Cabral

1924 - 1973

BORN IN BAFATA IN THE PORTUGUESE COLONY
of Guinea in 1924, Amilcar Cabral was a sensitive student
with a flair for writing. Guinea and Cape Verde Islands were
Portugal's sole 'possessions' in West Africa, and represented
the region's most oppressive colonial regime.

Portugal ruled through military might. Enforced labour
was still common and poverty was rife. The country was
undeveloped, and very few opportunities for advancement
were open to Africans.

In 1945, Cabral won a scholarship to study agronomy in
Lisbon, Portugal. Here he came into contact with students
from other Portuguese colonies in Africa - Angola and
Mozambique – and linked with their nationalist sentiments
regarding Portugal's brutal occupation of these countries. He
befriended Agostino Neto, a young medical student and
future leader of Angola. By the end of his studies in Lisbon
the sensitive young student had become politicised by the
idea of 'African-ness', and was determined to free his country
from the clutches of Portugal.

Returning to Guinea in 1952 as a qualified agronomist,
Cabral toured the country for two years carrying out an
agricultural survey for the Portuguese government. His
contact with villagers and rural communities was to prove
crucial in the years of struggle that lay ahead.

Between 1955 and 1959, Cabral travelled widely in
Europe, Africa, and China. In 1956, he worked for a time in
Angola where he witnessed first hand another Portuguese

colony's effort to resist oppression. Trained as a scientist, Cabral's approach to revolutionary thinking was methodical and persuasive. His study of peoples' struggles in Algeria, Cuba, China, and more recently in Ghana, led him to apply answers that were appropriate to the particular situation in Guinea and Cape Verde Islands. Portugal's vicious repression of a dock-workers' strike in Guinea in 1959 signalled the beginning of armed struggle for liberation. Cabral's African Party for the Independence of Guinea and Cape Verde (PAIGC) came out into the open.

In 1960 the PAIGC set up headquarters in neighbouring and newly independent Guinea, a former French colony of the same name. President Sekou Toure of Guinea became the PAIGC's most important ally. Conakry, the capital, was the recruiting point for young militants and exiles, who enlisted in the struggle. The Portuguese had never penetrated the Guinea hinterland. The politicisation of rural communities became Cabral's main strategy in the war against Portugal. Fighting a hit-and-run guerrilla operation that was to last thirteen years, the PAIGC under Cabral slowly eroded Portuguese control of most of the country. In the end, Portugal held only a few cities and armed garrisons. Along with the war of attrition, Cabral maintained a high level of diplomacy in the African and international community. By the late 1960's the PAIGC was recognised by the United Nations as the only legitimate representative of the people of the newly named Guinea-Bissau.

In 1974, the new nation gained independence from Portugal, but Amilcar Cabral never lived to see that day. Shot down by a party dissident in 1973, he is remembered as a revolutionary thinker and activist who liberated his country from foreign rule.

Malcolm X
1925 - 1965

DETROIT RED WAS A TEENAGER IN 'SWISH' clothes who loved the night life of Boston and New York in the 1940's. He frequented jazz clubs and dives, and soon graduated to street-hustling, dealing in drugs, prostitution, and guns. Many young Blacks in the big cities of northern USA found a career in crime. It seemed the best way to get even with a system that allowed them only the lowest jobs and worst living conditions. Detroit Red was just another casualty of the system – a young Black man living on the edge, often a fugitive from the law and from gangland bosses. In 1945, aged 20, he was arrested and brought to trial in Boston, convicted of robbery. He was sentenced to 10 years imprisonment.

Detroit Red was born Malcolm Little in 1925 in Omaha, America, son of a Baptist preacher and Garveyite, Earl Little. His mother, Louisa, was a fair-skinned woman. Malcolm's nickname was a reference to his light skin and red hair, and the fact that his family had lived in Detroit, Michigan. In 1931 when Malcolm was six years old, his father was found dead on railroad tracks, supposedly killed by white extremists who had earlier threatened his life. The Little family disintegrated after his death. Malcolm was a high-spirited youth with a knack for finding trouble. At the age of 12 he was put in a reform centre. At 14 he moved to Boston to live with his sister, and was intrigued by the big city lights. From Boston he moved on to New York and became Detroit Red, an underworld pimp, drug-peddler, and thief, whose number finally came up in 1945.

Malcolm X 1925 - 1965

During his prison term Malcolm underwent a remarkable conversion to Islam. Elijah Mohammed, an ex-Garveyite, had started the Black Muslim movement in America in the 1940's. Its extremist philosophy sometimes depicted Whites as devils, and Blacks as an original people whose time had come to achieve their destiny. Malcolm communicated with Elijah Mohammed from prison. He became his favourite pupil and the rising star of the Nation Of Islam, America's Black religio-militant movement. Malcolm had read widely while in prison. He had transformed himself into a conscious Black thinker, speaker, and activist.

After an early release from prison in 1952 Malcolm X (as he was now called) became the main speaker and organiser for the Nation Of Islam. A stirring orator who mixed street talk with his enlarged vocabulary, Malcolm was able to hustle for lost souls in the ghettoes where he himself had been a lost soul years earlier. Membership of the Nation Of Islam increased dramatically in the 1950's mainly due to its charismatic spokesman, Malcolm X, whose controversial and fluent style made him a media target wherever he travelled.

Diametrically opposed to Martin Luther King's non-violent style of protest, Malcolm X preached an eye for an eye and a tooth for a tooth – a message that young Blacks in the northern cities responded to. The Black revolution was entering a new phase. Confrontation seemed the only answer to centuries of recurrent oppression. Blacks, he preached, must form a separate nation in America or Africa. This was the only way to be independent and free.

By the early 1960's Malcolm X had made many enemies within and outside the movement. His popularity posed a threat to Elijah Mohammed's leadership and created jealousies within the Nation Of Islam. Malcolm was carpeted by Elijah for statements made after President Kennedy's death. The growing rift between the two men resulted in his leaving the Nation Of Islam in 1964. In that year he made his first visit to Mecca, a journey which radically altered his views regarding race, and broadened his perspective on world liberation struggles. From there he travelled to the Lebanon, Nigeria, Ghana, and Algeria, where large audiences turned out to hear the great African-American activist.

But his vision of a much broader revolutionary alliance never materialised. Hounded by the press for his extreme views, threatened with death because of his unequivocal stance, Malcolm X, now El-hajj Malik el-Shabazz, was shot by assassins as he addressed a public meeting in 1965. His writings and speeches became text-books for Black consciousness the world over.

Walter Rodney
1942 - 1980

ON JUNE 13TH 1980 A YOUNG MAN SAT IN A CAR in Georgetown, Guyana, testing a two-way device he had been given by an alleged electronics expert. The device, which concealed a bomb, exploded in his hands, killing yet another great Black leader and scholar. Dr. Walter Rodney, aged only 38, passed into history.

Walter Rodney was born in the British colony of Guyana in 1942. His father was involved in politics, and the young Walter often distributed leaflets for the PPP (People's Progressive Party) as an eleven year old. A brilliant student, he attended the University of the West Indies in Mona, Jamaica, where he graduated with honours in History in 1963. Rodney continued his studies in England where he received a Doctorate in African History at the School of Oriental & African Studies.

Leaving London in 1966, Dr. Walter Rodney taught History at the University of Dar Es Salaam in Tanzania. A year later, in 1967, he returned to Jamaica's Mona Campus to lecture in History. His teaching activities took him to the ghettoes of Kingston where he reasoned with the poorer masses of the society. His book *Grounding With My Brothers* is a revelatory account of his links with the Rastafari movement, whose cause he supported, and whose philosophy and lifestyle he helped to publicise. He was not afraid to admit that he had learnt from simple Black people who were considered illiterate. As a scholar he had broken the hallowed conventions of academia by grounding with the underprivileged. Rodney

Walter Rodney 1942 - 1980

was viewed by the authorities as subversive, and was refused re-entry to Jamaica after a brief visit to Canada in 1968. The government ban on Rodney sparked riots on the streets of Kingston, as ripples of Black Power spread throughout America and the Caribbean.

Dr. Walter Rodney returned to Tanzania where he taught history for the next six years. Dar Es Salaam was a focus for African revolutionary thought. Rodney's piercing analyses of history, class and struggle added a new dimension to Africa's fight against a new enemy – neo-colonialism. In 1974 Rodney returned to his native Guyana to take up an appointment as Chair of History at the local university. The Government of President Forbes Burnham blocked his appointment, but Rodney was determined to stay and support the workers' struggle against an increasingly oppressive regime.

In 1975, the Working People's Alliance (WPA) was formed, a coalition of socialist groups representing the working masses of Guyana, who were mainly of Asian and African origin. Inevitably Rodney emerged as one of the Party's leading figures. In the following years the WPA attracted disillusioned members of the country's two political parties. By the end of the decade it was a political force to be reckoned with.

When a mysterious fire burned down the headquarters of the ruling party, Rodney and other members of the WPA were arrested on the flimsiest evidence and charged with arson. A team of Caribbean lawyers rallied to his defence. On June 13th 1980, with the case against him still pending, Rodney was killed by a bomb, probably detonated by remote control.

Dr. Walter Rodney's searching analysis of First and Third World relationships is recorded in his major work *How Europe Underdeveloped Africa*. As a historian he offered new insights into the problems of post-independence Africa. As a revolutionary thinker and activist he was always prepared to apply the lessons of history and scholarship to the struggles of oppressed people the world over.

Bob Marley
1945 - 1981

IN 1945 ROBERT NESTA MARLEY WAS BORN IN the 'garden parish' of St. Ann's, Jamaica, to a White father and Black mother. From early youth he showed an outstanding talent for music and lyrical composition. Like many young Jamaicans he was attracted to the hypnotic rhythms of Rastafari culture, and its popular musical form, reggae. Musical stardom was often seen as the only escape-route from the poverty and frustration of ghetto-life in Jamaica.

In 1958 Bob moved to Trench Town in West Kingston where he lived for the next three years. Here he was inducted in the teachings of Rastafari by elders of the movement. He recalls these years with nostalgia in the classic *No Woman No Cry: I remember when we used to sit, In a government yard in Trench Town, And Georgie would make the fire light, Logwood burning through the night.*

In 1962 Bob Marley, with future reggae super-stars Peter McIntosh, Bunny Livingston, and the Barrett Brothers, formed the Wailers, the most successful musical ensemble ever to come out of Jamaica. The 'wail' of the sufferer was captured in everyday lyrics that fired the imagination of Black youths everywhere. His major albums *Catch a Fire, Talking Blues, Kaya, Burning an Illusion*, and *Exodus* contained revolutionary anthems that echoed the plight of Black communities worldwide. In *Talking Blues*, Bob sings 'I feel like bombing a church ... Now that I know the preacher is lying'. For over a decade the Wailers attracted huge audiences wherever they performed in Europe, America and the

Bob Marley 1945 - 1981

Caribbean. The reggae idiom reached out to world audiences, who were increasingly able to identify with Black struggle. The transcendent message of peace and love was couched in a cool, vibrant militancy. Its seductive rhythms inspired a post-war generation seeking answers to the pressures of modern life. The Wailers articulated the hope for a brave new world of equal rights and justice.

In the mid-1970's Bob Marley split from the Wailers to pursue a broader international career. He was widely seen as the prophet and spokesman of the Rastafari movement. His flowing dreadlocks and winning smile – featured on thousands of posters across the world – became a household symbol of liberation and social equity. His lyrics were the catchphrase of the masses. Though non-political, this diminutive musical genius wielded more authority and influence than Heads of State in the countries he visited. His rise to global fame was meteoric. By the late 1970's he was acclaimed from the Caribbean to Japan, from the Americas to Africa, from Europe to Australia and the Pacific Isles, as the premier ambassador of world peace and goodwill.

In December 1976 Bob Marley narrowly escaped an assassination attempt on his life, on the eve of the 'Smile Jamaica' concert. In 1978 he performed at the massive One Love Peace Concert in Jamaica, where he brought together the warring political factions led by Michael Manley and Edward Seaga, who joined hands with him on stage.

In 1980, at the highpoint of his career, he enthralled millions at Zimbabwe's independence celebrations. The lyrics of Africa Unite still echo hauntingly today: 'How good and how pleasant it would be / Before God and man / To see the unification / Of all Africans'.

Struck down by a mystery illness in 1980, Bob Marley slowly succumbed to the inevitable. His unshakeable faith in the brotherhood of man and the fatherhood of Ras Tafari

(Emperor Haile Selassie 1 of Ethiopia) sustained him throughout the long months of his tragic illness. In 1981 the world lost one of the leading lights of the 20th century. More than any other figure in the Rastafari movement he popularised a new culture that influenced the planet. He left a musical legacy that few can equal, but many can emulate. For millions of fans, followers and admirers, he has become a beacon in the darkness of Babylonian captivity.